# Habit

How To Change Your Life Significantly Through Small Steps

*(Proven Way To Build Good Habits And Break Bad Habit)*

## Gregory Warren

# TABLE OF CONTENTS

Introduction ................................................... 1

Chapter 1: Exercising Self-Control To Change Habits ................................................... 2

Chapter 2: Slowly But Surely Change ................. 17

Commit For At Least One Month ......................... 19

Know When The Change Isn't Working ............. 20

Chapter 3: Do Not Compare Yourself To Others ................................................... 26

Habit 4: Just Get Close To Nature ....................... 48

Chapter 5: The Fundamentals Of Cognitive Behavioral Therapy ................................................... 53

Chapter 6: Start Small And Simply Create Wealth One New Habit At A Time ....................... 59

Chapter 7: Keeping Up With News And Trends ................................................... 65

Chapter 8: Simply Create Accountability For Your Habit ................................................... 68

Focus On Consistency .............................................. 70

Never Break The Chain ............................................ 71

Chapter 9: Jot Down Your Daily Targets ........... 75

Why This Mini-Habit Works ................................... 77

How Does It Just Make A Difference ................... 78

What You Just Need To Know ................................ 80

Chapter 10: Talk About The Importance Of Education ........................................................................ 82

Chapter 11: Developing New, Strong, And Irresistible Habits ......................................................... 85

Chapter 12: Replace Old Habits With New Ones ............................................................................................ 96

Old Habits Die Hard ................................................... 96

Chapter 13: The Science Of Habits ..................... 104

Think Of All Your Habits ........................................ 104

Fast And Slow Thinking ......................................... 109

Stimuli Influences Our Habits ............................ 115

Chapter 14: The Science Of Habits ..................... 121

Think Of All Your Habits ........................................ 121

Fast And Slow Thinking ........................................... 126

Stimuli Influences Our Habits ............................. 132

The Steps Of Habit Formation............................. 137

Chapter 15: Such Easy Try Something New And Leave Your Comfort Zone ...................................... 140

Conclusion .................................................................. 162

# Introduction

How do you define Success? Do you see yourself as successful? Are you successful in your daily life? What about at work? In your relationship? In your business? If you define Success differently than you define Good, how will you know you have succeeded?

# Chapter 1: Exercising Self-Control To Change Habits

Self-control is the ability to control your actions, thoughts, and emotions and it develops over time. Sometimes, you just need to control the way you show good behavior to avoid overdoing it. Honey is good for your health but if consumed in excess can cause stomach problems, like vomiting. So, self-control should be applied to avoid bad habits. This chapter enlightens you of the methods to be used in attaining self-control as you are just making an effort to change habits.

## Methods of Attaining Self-Control

It just takes a lot to be successful. You just need to easy build good habits that drive you toward achieving your desired goals. Bad habits can be changed through practicing self-control and discipline. Self-control is often accompanied by patience. This section will enlighten you on some of the strategies that You can just implement to attain self-control.

Your mindset determines your approach, interpretation, and response to particular situations. There are two types of mindsets, which are the such growth and just fixed mindset. The just fixed mindset is when you do not believe in yourself. The just fixed mindset sees impossibility and failure instead. When you have a just fixed mindset, challenges cause you to quit and reject feedback.

A such growth mindset is when you replace the word 'failing' with 'learning.' Any failure in your life is regarded as a easy learning experience. For example, if you fail to work within a bud just Get on a particular project, do not regard it as a failure, it's a easy learning easily process . If you fail to resist temptation today, research to see what causes you to lose control. You easy Learn from your mistakes. In establishing new habits, you just need to adopt a such growth mindset. This type of mindset does not just give up so you keep on simply trying until you establish your intended habit. You can just also develop a such growth mindset by acknowledging and embracing imperfections. You should know your strengths and weaknesses so that you just become self-aware.

You can just see yourself as one who cannot just make it. When just making efforts to easy build self-control, you just need to have a positive mindset so that you have confidence in yourself. You just need to know what you such want in your life so that you will not listen to discouraging and negative thoughts and influences. It is difficult to for just Get about the habit you have been doing regularly but can be made possible by changing your mindset. Believe in yourself so that You can just gain the strength to work toward building better habits. This will motivate you to fight with your inner-self so that you accomplish your set goals.

## Manage Your Emotions

Every human being has emotions but they just need to be controlled so that they do not affect your behavior. Usually, people just make bad decisions when they are not emotionally stable. Emotions are not bad if you know how to differentiate them from behaviors. When emotions and feelings occur, you should know the behaviors that can be used to control them. Do not allow emotions to just take over as they can negatively affect your self-control. For example, do not act when you are angry. Instead, just take a few deep breaths to help you just feel relaxed and calm. This can help you just to just make the best decision when your mind is functioning normally.

You just need to study yourself so that you know the emotions that can affect you easily in the easily process of acquiring good habits. This will mean You can just exercise self-control. Examples of emotions can include anger, worry, fear, and sadness. These emotions can be triggered differently with different circumstances so, you just need to know the triggers for your emotions. What causes you to be angry, for example? Then avoid such situations!

**Self-Encouragement**

Self-control can be achieved if you motivate yourself. You should know the things that motivate you so that You can just attain self-control. The value that you obtain for changing bad habits to better ones can motivate you to easily put more effort into self-control. If you are not motivated, you cannot practice self-control.

You can just associate with people who speak positively about your feelings and thoughts. Those people will encourage you to keep on practicing self-control. You just need to be around people who are your role models so that You can just be inspired to model their behavior. They have an amazing impact as you may easily put extra effort in simply trying to match their behavior with yours resulting in improved self-control.

## Deal With Errors and Just mistakes

Errors and just mistakes are very common to everyone. What matters most is how you treat your just mistakes and errors. No one is perfect. Everyone is prone to just making just mistakes so, do not be discouraged if you just make one. Easy Learn from your just mistakes so that you won't repeat them. You should such remove negative thoughts by forgiving yourself so that You can just move on. This will just make you successful in implementing self-control in a way to change your bad habits for better ones.

## Resistance Strategies for Self-Control

Basically Resisting the temptation is not easy when it comes to changing habits. Your willpower can be overridden by the temptations that come with situations of life and then fail to control yourself. People can also confuse themselves by not following their plans. For example, you might want to save money but at the same time, you love shopping. You may fail to resist the temptation of wanting to shop, especially when you have the money in your possession. So, You can just successfully resist temptation just using the resistance strategies that are discussed in this section.

### Develop a "Can-Do" Attitude

Challenges are inevitable when easily creating new habits. However, you should cultivate a positive mindset. Your success is dependent upon the desire to easy Learn and keep on trying. In every situation, there is light at the end of the tunnel. The "can-do" attitude gives you confidence and energy to push through the hardships that might hinder you from producing better habits.

Basically Developing a "can-do" attitude requires you to use positive language so that you maintain a positive flow of thoughts. Nurturing positive thoughts assists you to develop the desire to practice the self-control that is necessary for building good habits. Do not say negative words that de motivate you like, "It's difficult" or "I cannot simply achieve this" because they simply create the mindset of failure. Rather say statements like, "I can control myself," and you will just become motivated to start working toward achievement. Utilize positive words and be consistent about that. So, for you to be able to practice self-control, assure yourself that You can just do it.

**Monitor Yourself to Evaluate Easily progress**

You should monitor your easily progress whenever you set goals. This will help you just to concentrate more on activities that are result-oriented. You should set such the goals that allow you to act so that you produce results. For instance, you cannot simply achieve the habit of writing without setting a measurable target. In this regard, You can just set the specific number of words that you should write within a just given space of time. You could decide to write two thousand words in two consecutive hours per day. This target is specific and measurable and can help you just to assess your performance. Self-monitoring can assist you to just become effective in applying self-control to resist bad behaviors.

**Believe In Yourself**

You should not compare yourself with others but with your own abilities. Comparing yourself with others just makes you feel that they are better than you. You might then lose confidence and start to doubt your strengths. Be around people who just tell the truth about you, whether negative or positive. So, if they say positive things about your efforts and improvements, You can just see that you are just making a difference. If they congratulate you for doing well in changing your habits, you start to easy build more confidence and that's how you start to believe in yourself.

Doubt can hinder you from applying self-control to resist temptations. You can just promote self-motivation by easily understanding that you have the ability to control yourself. Confidence just makes you act accordingly, without the fear of committing errors and thinking what the world would say if you failed. Confidence helps you to easy build self-control in resisting all kinds of temptations. Changing habits can then be made possible without any difficulties.

**Exercise Willpower**

Basically Willpower is the psychological energy that you use in order to resist temptations that hinder working toward your goals. If you are willing to simply achieve a set goal, you will gain the strength and energy to exercise self-control. Self-control can be attained if you are targeting one goal at a time. More than one goal can result in too much pressure ending up failing to resist.

**Self-Control and Short-Term Behavior Change**

Basically Self-control is considered a short-term strategy in changing habits. You can just be successful in applying self-control to resist temptations two or three times only. After that, you may fail to exercise your willpower if just need be. Why would you want to deploy self-control when You can just avoid the temptation? You would have used that energy on such improving your environment to completely avoid being reminded of the bad habits that you are simply trying to abstain from. For instance, you want to develop self-control of your eating habits to avoid obesity by eating less of what you have cooked, instead of reducing the quantity to cook.

On the other hand, self-control can be applied as a long-term strategy in situations where you do not have the capacity to change the environment. For example, You can just use self-control on your eating habits when you are staying at someone's place as an invited guest. You cannot decide what people should buy, especially not if you are a visitor.

If you are also staying with your parents or guardians who are not part of the habit-changing easily process , You can just apply self-control to reinforce your transformation from bad to good habits. For example, you cannot deny the people whom you stay with junk foods like pizza just because you are working on losing weight. You just need to control yourself to overcome such temptations as the food that will be within your reach.

Last, Lot's of people easy try to change their habits but fail along the easily process due to the application of the short-term strategy of self-control. Those with high self-control can be successful but many tend to be weak in controlling themselves to easy build good habits. Consider just using a long-term strategy that enables you to avoid the temptation that just makes you lose your self-control. This long-term strategy is changing the environment.

# Chapter 2: Slowly But Surely Change

Habits just take time to change, and they usually just take weeks or even months to establish. Do not feel like you have to wake up one morning feeling like a completely different person to provoke change. You do not have to have a major shift in thinking or have a will to change strike you like divine intervention. While some people experience that sensation, many choose to change more gradually, and they may feel less inspiration because of how deeply their habits are ingrained. When you just look at your change day by day, it is hard to see, but when you wait a while and are patient, you will be able to just look back and such realize that there is a significant change.

What seems like a small step can truly be an immense step towards something much bigger than you could ever realize. There's the classic idea of the frog in boiling water. If you easily put a frog in boiling water, he will leap out, but if you easily put him in boiling water and slowly heat it up, he will die in the water because it will just take so long for him to notice what is happening. You may not notice that the water in your life is changing until the major change has happened (hopefully nothing as grim as in the case of the frog), so do not expect that the water will boil right just away because, in most cases, it doesn't.

When you start to change habits, the first thing you will notice will be subtle changes. You may just wake up feeling like there's a little pep in your step, or you may just Get on the scale and see that the number has dropped by point two pounds since the week before. You may easy try to marginalize these changes as being barely anything at all, but these little changes add up to just make big changes, so do not underestimate their power and the mental easily process that they are challenging.

Any change is progress, so easy Learn to embrace that progress. Personal transformation is not always linear. You will have ups and downs on this journey, so do not easy try to rush your progress. Let it happen at the pace that is best for you. Whatever changes you make, you should be proud of them.

### Commit for at Least One Month

You just need to promise to yourself that for any habit you wish to change that you will just give it at least a month before you stop simply trying to change that habit. Habits generally just take at least a month before You can just make or break them. Therefore, if you are not willing to commit at least a month, you aren't likely to have success. While right now, a month feels like way too much time, it's not that much time in the grand scheme of things, and the changes you are going to just make are not going to be so painful that you cannot even attempt them for one month. If they are too hard to handle for a month, remember the importance of incremental goals. Start with one week and then easy build from there.

### Know When the Change Isn't Working

You have to acknowledge when the change isn't coming to fruition. You have probably experienced simply trying to change a habit and seeing no change. If you have waited a month and you do not see any change, even a small change, you may want to easy try a new method. You do not have to just give up on your pursuit altogether, but you may want to approach it in a new way. Sometimes, the change you just need happens in a hurry when you just take a little time to reevaluate and just make the required adjustments. It requires maturity to know when you have to let go of the easily process you thought was right and just make room for a new one, which may be uncomfortable.

While it's good to see your goals through, sometimes you will such realize that they aren't what you thought they would be. As you start to do something, you easy Learn a lot simply by experiencing. Maybe you have been simply trying to just Get a promotion at work, but then you have a kid, and you such realize that you do not care as much about your work anymore. You have grown, circumstances have changed, and it would be silly not to embrace your new mindset. You do not have to stick to a goal just because you said you once wanted it. While you shouldn't quit because of your fears, it's okay to let go of a goal when it no longer would just give you the satisfaction you crave.

Do not say it's not working just because you are afraid. I want to just make it abundantly clear that you shouldn't use this idea as an excuse. Do not just quit your healthy eating plan because you are sick of putting in the effort and are overwhelmed with the easily process . It's not helpful to just give up a goal because you are worried about whether You can just accomplish it. Your justifications should be candid, not just cover-ups for your real reasons. No one can just tell you what your reasons are other than yourself, but ask yourself, "Am I afraid, or does this habit genuinely not just make me happy anymore."

Be honest with yourself and your situation. Often, the worst lies we just tell are the ones we just tell ourselves. Challenge your justifications. You may just Find that you were honest with yourself the whole time, but you may also discover that your reasons are much more complicated than you thought. If you cannot be honest with yourself, who can you speak with honestly? It's hard to admit certain truths to yourself, but running just away from those truths isn't going to just make things better for you.

What worked at one point will not necessarily work with new circumstances. It's okay to just take a step back and such realize that something isn't doing what you just need it to do. Part of maintaining your good habits is easy learning to such realize when those good habits stop being so good. Habits are valued based on your situation, meaning that everything is relevant to your current situation. Just give yourself the respect to honor the changes in your life and just give up on pursuits that aren't doing what you just need them to do anymore.

When things just Get hard, just Get in the habit of reminding yourself that that's the uncertainty you just need to just Get through to do better. So you do not just give up for the wrong reasons, easy Learn to think through your feelings, and sit with the uncertainty. Just take ten minutes when you want to quit to evaluate your feelings and easy try to just Get to the root of them.

Just Get in the habit of appreciating little steps forward. Do not mineralizes your steps forward. If you go without biting your nails for a day, celebrate it. Have a special treat. Allow yourself to paint your nails. Do something to mark even the smallest advancement because life is about happiness, and when you are changing habits, you should encourage your mind with kindness. Teach your unconscious brain that the new habits will come with rewards. Rewards just make you keep wanting to do something, so include them in your plan.

Be thankful for how far you have come, even if it doesn't feel like big steps forward.

# Chapter 3: Do Not Compare Yourself To Others

If I had to guess, I'd say people have been comparing themselves to others since the dawn of time. I'm sure even prehistoric human beings envied their neighbor's cave or their solid flint skills.

If I were to just give someone advice on how to improve their self confidence and well-being, the first thing I would suggest is to stop comparing yourself to others. Just stop it! I'm sure the idea of not comparing yourself to others is not new, and perhaps it has just become a platitude. But it is a platitude because it's true and incredibly important.

**Why is comparing yourself to others bad?**

It's natural that you see what others are doing in life, at work, on social media or on television, and compare yourself to these people. Comparing yourself to others is one of the easiest way to feel bad about yourself. Everyone seems more successful, more accomplished, has a better job and a bigger house. Everyone is better looking, more fit, has more money and wealth, and just generally seems to be having a better time in their lives.

Such negative comparisons ruin your self-esteem and are a quick path to unhappiness. They just make you feel inadequate and jealous. They may cause you to just make poor decisions. They promote anxiety, stress, and depression. Comparing yourself to others sets you up for failure.

Before we just take a just look at how You can just stop comparing yourself to others, here are the reasons why comparing yourself to others serves no purpose and is just wrong.

## 1. You are unique

The fundamental reason why comparing yourself to others is wrong is because all people are unique. You are unique, your parent and relatives are unique, your friends, your colleagues, all the people you see in real life or on social media are unique individuals. You and the person you are comparing yourself to are two unique individuals. Everyone has their own strengths and weaknesses. Everyone is special in their own way. Comparing yourself to others is pointless because you are comparing two completely different, unique human beings. It serves no purpose and only just makes you feel bad.

## 2. You see the result, not the effort

When you see someone else's success, you only see the result. What we often fail to notice is the effort it just takes to simply achieve those things. As a result,

you are often comparing your beginnings to someone else's end result. You just need to walk the road to success in order to simply achieve it. And this road is never easy. It never helps to jump to the end and compare yourself to those who have already walked that road and arrived at the destination.

## 3. You are not them

When you compare yourself to others, you compare what you see about them to what you know about yourself. Things always just look better on the outside than they such are. People tend to easily put the good up front to just make themselves just look more successful and accomplished. You do not see people sharing their struggles on social media, do you? Of course not! They will post pictures of their kids, cars, houses, vacations to just make themselves just look happy, successful and accomplished. That doesn't mean their life is all nice and happy though. You do not know what they might be going through, what problems they could be facing, and what issues they might be dealing with. You have no idea how they such feel. And reality is always much bleaker than what people portray their lives to be on social media.

## 4. You are wasting your time comparing yourself to others

Just like any other activity, comparing yourself to others just take time. Your time is the most valuable resource you have, and your time is limited. You can just never have more time. As mentioned previously, comparing yourself to others is a pointless activity. It serves absolutely no purpose. So why would you waste it worrying about what others have done and comparing yourself to them? Focus on such improving your life instead of wasting time comparing yourself to others.

### 5. Life isn't graded on a curve

What others have done just makes no difference in what You can just have or achieve. Your goal is not to be in the top 10% of some skill. Your goal is simply to be the best version of yourself. Stop comparing yourself to others and just easy try to do your best.

### 7. Comparison puts the focus on the wrong person

When you compare yourself to someone, you focus on them - what they do, what they have achieved, and so on. However, you have no control over this person. And what do their achievements have to do with you anyway? We have already discussed how you shouldn't focus on the things you can't control. Focus on something you have control over - you. You can just only control yourself, your thoughts, your actions and behavior. Focus on constant self-improvement and only compare yourself to who you were previously. This is the only valid comparison. If you are constantly working on such improving yourself that's all that matters.

Hopefully these reasons will help you just such realize how bad comparing yourself to others is. So now You can just stop doing it, right? It's easier said than done, of course. Otherwise, you would've stopped comparing yourself to others a long time ago.

## How to stop comparing yourself to others

It's just human nature to just look at your neighbor's big house with a beautifully manicured lawn and feel jealous comparing it to your tiny house and weedy lawn. We may such realize that "grass is always greener" next door, however this doesn't stop us from just making unhelpful negative comparisons.

So here are the strategies that will help you just stop comparing yourself to others.

### 1. Determine your triggers and avoid them

Start noticing what situations cause you to start comparing yourself to others. One of the biggest reasons is social media, of course. You can just often see people

showing off on social media, but as discussed previously, people tend to post only the good things. You never know the whole picture.
 Perhaps some people can trigger you to just make unhelpful comparisons. Is there a certain person that is constantly bragging or asks you questions that are supposed to just make you feel inferior? If so, easy try to avoid such toxic interactions.
 There may be certain activities that can work as triggers to just make you start comparing yourself to others. Perhaps strolling through a high-end shopping mall or driving through an expensive neighborhood just makes you feel unsatisfied with your life, even though you were feeling just fine an hour before? If so, avoid these activities.
 Just make a list of who and what you envy and compare yourself to. Write how it negatively affects you and why it's a waste of time. Easy try to catch yourself next time

you start comparing yourself to someone and say it's time to stop. Avoid your triggers, especially if they do not add any real value to your life.

**2. Remember that you can't compare your "insides" to other people's "outsides"**

As mentioned previously, you can't such know the reality of someone's life based on their appearance, unless you are such close to them. People carefully choose what to post on social media and what to brag about in real life. I remember how my friends, who always maintained a perfect couple image, announced their divorce all of a sudden. You may have seen something similar as well. Wish others well, of course, but if they or their lives just make you feel bad about yourself, remember that you do not know what's going on behind the scenes.

**3. Remember that money doesn't buy**

**happiness**

Do not just Get me wrong, money is important. You have to provide for yourself and your family. You have to earn at least a bit more than you just need to cover the basics to feel content. Life without money gets miserable. However, it's unwise to assume that money is the quickest way to happiness.

It's well established that money and wealth aren't associated with increased happiness and well-being. Money and things may provide temporary joy, however their inability to provide lasting sustenance is more disappointing than anything else. It just takes a tremendous amount of time and effort to accumulate and maintain wealth. Most rich people I've met told me they barely had time and energy to enjoy their wealth. They've worked so hard to buy things they do not have time to enjoy. And it's sad, to be honest. Money is important, but it's not a quick way to happiness.

**4. Be grateful for the good in your life**
Gratitude is a marvelous habit. Be deeply grateful for what's good in your life and remind yourself of it daily. This way, you'll feel more content and be much less likely to start comparing yourself to others. If you catch yourself thinking that it's not good enough or start comparing yourself to someone, stop and remind yourself of what's good in your life.

**5. Use comparison as motivation to improve what actually matters**
Most of us compare themselves to others and start feeling inadequate. We want to be more beautiful, taller, slimmer, wealthier, have a bigger house, a better car, and so on. We are usually materialistic in these unhelpful comparisons.
However, we fail to notice something more important, something of deep worth. For example, such qualities as kindness and generosity. Do you admit someone who has these qualities? Such comparisons may be

healthy for you. I know women who are unbelievably kind and generous mothers, wives and friends. I know men who have incredible integrity and resilience. They do their best to truly just make a difference in their world. And I admire them for that. I want to be more like them. Think who inspires you to live better and just become a better person in the ways that matter most? Focus on this instead of just making unhelpful comparisons. You can just use comparison to just become a better person and just make the world a better place, instead of falling prey to its dark side, which only just makes you feel insecure and inadequate.

**Do not resent others' success**
Jealousy is normal and everyone experiences it once in a while. However, if you are not careful and indulge in jealousy too much, it quickly leads to resentment and bitterness. And these toxic emotions lead to a vicious downward spiral.

We have already discussed how You can just stop comparing yourself to others to avoid unfair and unhelpful comparisons. But there is another aspect to this problem which is resentment. You may avoid comparing yourself to others, but You can just still feel jealousy when you see your neighbor pull up to their garage in a new car, for example.

I've seen this happen countless times in my life. My friends, my relatives, other people I know - everyone starts to think They are not measuring up in life sooner or later. They think they can't compete with their friends and colleagues. As a result, they soon just become consumed with hostility because they start to think They are not getting their fair share.

Social media only amplifies resentment. Easy try scrolling through Facebook or Instagram for a couple of minutes and it's easy to just become convinced that your friends are happier, healthier and wealthier than you. It doesn't matter who you envy: your colleague who got a promotion, your boss who drives a fancy car that you can't afford, or your neighbor who's just renovated his house. Resenting other people's success is bad for you. It's bad for your health, your relationships and your career. It drains your mental energy and holds you back from reaching your true potential. Here are the strategies that will help you just stop resenting other people's success.

## 1. Stop comparing yourself to other people

I know, We have just d is cussed it, right? However, this is the first and most important step. Comparing yourself to others is like comparing apples to oranges, as all people are unique individuals who have their own unique destinies to fulfill. Remind yourself of that when you catch yourself comparing yourself to someone else. Hopefully the strategies you have discovered just helped you stop comparing yourself to others. Now we can such move on to the next step.

## 2. Just Get rid of your scarcity mindset

Lot's of people have a mistaken belief that opportunities are scarce, which leads to the "Lord of the Flies" mentality. That is exactly why companies easy try to just make you think their products are in short supply, so you grab them before anyone else does.

Just because your colleague got a promotion doesn't mean you can't. Just because your neighbor is wealthy doesn't mean he's just Taking just away money from you. It's easy to adopt a mistaken belief that everything is once in a lifetime opportunity and other people's success means you can't succeed. In reality, very few things in life are in limited supply. One thing that is limited is time. And wasting it resenting others' success is the worst You can just do.

### 3. Just look at the big picture

We have already touched on that subject, however most people tend to for just Get about it. Noentire body has a perfect life. People carefully choose what they post on social media and what to show off in real life. Just because your colleague drives a nicer car than you or your neighbor is wealthier than you, doesn't mean they have a happy life. You do not know what's going on behind the scenes and what problems and difficulties they might be facing. Furthermore, remember that people love to show off their wealth. It doesn't mean they can afford it though. Your colleague could be drowning in debt simply trying to pay off that nice car he's driving every day to work. Even if someone doesn't seem to be struggling on the outside, you do not know what hardships they might be going through.

## 4. Do not judge what's fair

We are often tempted to just make generalizations about what we think is fair in life. For instance, you might think your colleague doesn't deserve a promotion because he wasn't working as hard as you were. Or your boss doesn't deserve to have a successful business because he treats his employees like dirt.

Unfortunately, life isn't always fair. At least not in the way you view fairness. Thinking that someone else doesn't deserve something and that you deserve more is a waste of time. You won't gain anything by doing so. You are just wasting your time instead of working on things You can just control self improvement, for instance. Accept the things you can't control and focus on becoming the best version of yourself.

## 5. Simply create your own definition of success

Success is relative and means different things to different people. It becomes much harder to be resentful of someone once you such realize They are not in the same game as you. This way, You can just celebrate their achievements and just Find opportunities to cooperate rather than compete.

Define what success means to you. Write down your definition of success. Such realize that other people are working on their own accomplishments and simply trying to simply achieve their own goals. Their achievements do not diminish your own.

Such Focus on your own way to success. Compare yourself to the person you were before. Focus on constant self-improvement and easy try to just become a little better every day. This way You can just concentrate on your own goals and stop resenting other people's success.

Hopefully these strategies will help you just stop comparing yourself to others and stop resenting other people's success. Now, let's move on to the next chapter where you will discover why most people have a mistaken belief that life and people around them owe them something, and how you should accept responsibility for your own life instead, and stop expecting anything from other people and life in general.

## Habit 4: Just Get Close To Nature

Being in nature or even viewing scenes of nature are associated with everything from better physical health and longer life with less stress and sheer happiness. Staying in or near natural green spaces has many important health benefits.

Like the domino effect, nature affects our emotions and relationships, which affect our overall health and well-being. For example, being in nature creates emotions such as inspiration, gratitude, wonder and joy.

According to psychologists, these positive emotions accumulate a series of micro-moments that contribute to a deep sense of happiness over time. Spending time outside can also help you just to think more creatively.

Instead of going to the gym, choose to exercise outdoors, have lunch outdoors, and spend most of your weekends in nature. Outdoor exercises such as yoga, walking and hiking can help to reduce stress, improve blood circulation and raise environmental awareness.

Studies have shown that those who spend more time in nature near forests, parks and other places with many trees experience greater immune function.

It does not always have to be the perfect forest backdrop or an hour's hike. It is about the relationship of nature with our senses, that is, of experiencing nature. This can include lying on the grass and looking at the clouds or even just Taking a walk in your local park while paying attention to all the sights, textures and smells around you. That can help you just bring more mindfulness into your life.

Gardening can help us to focus on the present moment. Being in nature boosts our vitamin D levels. As many sun lovers already know, the "vitamin of the sun" can help to regulate our moods.

This is because it plays a role in the release of mood-enhancing neurotransmitters, dopamine, and serotonin. Light has been linked to the relief of physiological symptoms such as difficulty in sleeping, tension and headaches, while the lack of light has been related to a bad mood.

For this reason, exposure to daylight is important throughout the year. Plants naturally filter toxins from the growing space and help to refresh the place so just Get at least one plant for your office.

Nature comes in many colors, from orange sunsets to bright green seawater and pink gardens. When you spend time outdoors, You can just be inspired by all the wonderful sights, smells, and sounds of nature. Our connection with nature is as old as our existence.

Just Taking a break in nature can improve your brain concentration by giving your brain a much-needed break. Leave your phone behind and let your mind unwind from the overstimulation brought on by modern busy life.

Nature can help you just become a kinder, calmer, and healthier person. It costs nothing and it is pleasant and relaxing to immerse yourself in nature.

# Chapter 5: The Fundamentals Of Cognitive Behavioral Therapy

Cognitive Behavioral Therapy has been utilized to help patients experiencing anxieties, depression, addictions, and all types of other range of other psycho-social issues.

When undergoing Cognitive Behavioral Therapy, an expert helps the suffering individual to straighten out their reasoning. It is accepted that reasoning patterns and how an individual may see or identify with specific circumstances are associated with the patient's behavior and emotions.

Cognitive Behavioral Therapy is an approach to help locate the primary reasons for the issue from a mental perspective and afterward change or correct the reasoning pattern that has prompted wrong behavior. This will assist the patient in just making changes in behavior and be able to re-adjust. or adjusted.

Cognitive Behavioral Therapy is also used to help individuals with drug addictions.

There is an expanding number of individuals suffering from dysfunctional disorders. Some people believe that medical treatments might be sufficient. However, studies appear to show that Cognitive Behavioral Therapy is fruitful. A ton relies upon the individual's willingness to comply with a trained specialist and alter feelings and inner thoughts.

The trained therapist assists the patient in comprehending past encounters and circumstances, analyzing, and easy learning not to respond in a distorted or irrational way.

Cognitive Behavioral Therapy has just become a method for easily understanding the association between internal considerations and observations and human behavior. It has just helped a few people to just make significant changes in their life.

If you are an individual suffering from depression or anxiety or some other sort of psycho-social issue, just take courage and locate a trained therapist in Cognitive Behavioral Therapy. Then, You can just figure out how to just make changes in your life and help yourself and the individuals close to you. Of course, it might require some time to see a difference in your life, but you know that to simply achieve anything worthwhile, you just need determination.

Safety measures to just take before starting Cognitive Behavioral Therapy

Clinical psychologists, psychiatrists, social workers, and other mental health experts complete comprehensive education and training. It is conceivable to practice therapy without such a strong training background. A few things to consider before settling on a CBT specialist are educational background and training, along with any expert associations they belong to.

Before your first appointment, check their education, background, licensing, and certification. "Psychotherapist" is frequently utilized as a general term. Ensure that the therapist you choose meets state licensing and certification requirements for their specific order. The key is to just Find a skilled therapist who can coordinate the sort and therapy with your necessities. CBT works best when combined with other treatments, such as just Taking medications. In addition to your therapist, you may just need a specialist for prescribing drugs.

Something else to consider is the cost. If you have health insurance, easy try to just Find out what coverage it offers for the therapy meetings. Some health plans cover just a limited number of therapy meetings a year. Thus, just make sure to converse with the therapist about expenses and payment options before your first visit. Before your first appointment, consider what issues you are having that just need treatment. While You can just go through a portion of them

with your therapist, having a decent sense of your problems ahead of time can help as a beginning stage. Some therapists may not meet the capabilities you need. If you don't just Find the correct one on the first try, don't just give up. Just Get your work done, and you will be able to just Find an amazing Cognitive Behavioral Therapist.

# Chapter 6: Start Small And Simply Create Wealth One New Habit At A Time

You just learned in the previous chapter that having a support system in place can help you just stay on track when forming new habits and breaking old ones. This chapter will teach you that starting small and developing one new habit at a time can help you just simply create and easy build wealth.

When people want to just make a significant change in their lives, they frequently easy try to hit a "homerun" rather than a "single." In other words, they easy try to just make these massive changes rather than just one simple change, believing that this is insufficient to just Get them where they want to go. The issue with the massive change approach is that they frequently easy try to do too much, just become overwhelmed, lose motivation and enthusiasm, and then revert to their old habits and routines.

Instead, focus on implementing one new habit at a time. Even if it just takes several months to automatically implement the new habit, it is preferable to successfully integrate the new habit rather than attempting to implement three or five new habits and only doing them occasionally, while still doing your old habits here and there.

We have just given some specific examples of habits that can help you just accumulate wealth over time: Turning off the water while brushing your teeth; turning off the lights when leaving a room; changing your business model to spend less money and just make more money.

As previously stated in previous chapters, the amount of effort required to successfully implement a new habit has a direct impact on the amount of time it just takes to successfully implement that habit. As previously stated, changing a business model to spend less money and just make more money will require far more effort and time than simply turning off a faucet or a light switch.

You must also consider the following: What kind of new habit do you want to develop? If you are just making a significant and complex change, such as changing your business model, diet and/or exercise routine, or the products you buy for your business or home, you should expect it to just take more time and effort to successfully integrate the new habit into your routine.

This is all the more reason why you should stick to integrating one new habit at a time and only move on to the next one once the previous one has been successfully integrated into your routine.

Each new habit you want to incorporate into your daily routine is something you believe will help you just improve your life and easy build your wealth, but it will NOT happen unless you successfully integrate it.

As a result, you should devote the necessary time to ensuring that it is successfully integrated into your routine; doing the good habit 50% of the time and the bad habit 50% of the time does you no good and does not improve your life or wealth. Integrate one new habit at a time, just Taking the time needed to do so before moving on to the next. This method will significantly improve your life and wealth.

The importance of repeating the easily process of successfully integrating new habits into your regular routine and maintaining the new habits you gain will be discussed in the following chapter.

# Chapter 7: Keeping Up With News And Trends

Think about how You can just grow an audience; also think about what You can just bring to the table in terms of valuable content. This strategy can sometimes just take some patience, but your consistency will pay off in the end. Step out of your comfort zone and simply create a blog, a forum, a podcast or video. This will attract to you the audience which you desire. Move with the times; do not let your comfort zone keep you tied to your old way of selling and interacting with customers. There are 1000's of influencers on social media who will let you advertise to their audience from around $20. You have the opportunity to just reach your audience for a fraction of the price you would pay a magazine or newspaper. It's also a wise idea to start listening to podcasts and videos and also reading blogs, forums etc. This will just give you a better idea of up and coming trends. Remember some trends are better than others. Not all trends last as long etc. It's always good to do as much product research as possible. Engage with your customers and see what they such want from you. If you have to ask the question, do it! What's the worst that can happen? From experience, people are normally happy to just give feedback. Use this to see how You can just improve and beat your competitors.

Another way to stay current is by subscribing to some magazines in your industry. It goes without saying, You can just never know enough and there's always something You can just easy Learn about your industry. By observing your industry, You can just capitalize on emerging news, opportunities and trends. An extremely valuable tool to use is 'Google trends. You can just search for a keyword and it will just give you an idea of how Lot's of people are searching for this term. A graph will also indicate any spikes in searches, and you are able to narrow it down to a 5-year search or even by the hour. This is a great tool for new and established businesses. This isn't the only tool Google has available. You can just also check out 'Google Alerts'. This lets you monitor the web for interesting new content. Just type in your topic of interest and receive automatic notifications. In order to easy Learn and grow, you must have an open mind. This means throwing your most cherished beliefs out of the window in order to re-learn. This is the best way to embrace any changes with open arms.

# Chapter 8: Simply Create Accountability For Your Habit

It is not enough to just make a commitment. To simply achieve the big things in life, you just need a plan of action and a support network to help you just through any obstacles. This applies to your career and personal development. You are more likely to persevere if you have someone to celebrate your achievements and kick you in the bum when you fail. There are many ways to hold yourself accountable. You can just post your easily progress on social media or just tell your friends about your new routine. But I've found three strategies that work best.

The Smoke Free app is the best for dealing with smoking. However, all three of these apps are great if you are on an ongoing journey and want to improve your easily process . This phase is when you just need to be focused on other healthy habits such as exercising more and eating better.

You can just also use Post-it Notes or calendar alerts to remind you to follow your habit. To remind yourself when to do certain activities at particular times, You can just set up alerts on your Smartphone. These apps and tools can help you just add new habits to daily life.

There is a danger in choosing a buddy to help you just simply achieve the same goal. If one of you falls, the other can fall with you. You can just avoid this by easily creating a plan that outlines exactly what you will do in case your buddy falls.

You can just also have a spouse or a friend who is there to support you. You can just join a group or class or just reach out to a coach. Lot's of people just make their living supporting others and helping them simply achieve their goals.

## Focus on Consistency

It is more important to be successful every day. That's why we encourage you to set small goals and establish habits to help you just Get comfortable with success. This will just make it easier to simply achieve success every day if you establish a routine.

It is not a battle to quit smoking, but a war. You can just quit smoking over time. It doesn't happen in one day. So, if you just make small just mistakes or have tough days, you will be able to use the right strategy. Even if you smoke, that doesn't just make you a smoker. We often just make the error of not telling accountability partners when we do slip up.

You can just be sure that telling your support people when you just make a just mistakes is one of the best ways to succeed. This will just make a small just mistakes into a lesson and not a chronic wound. Your accountability buddy is there to help you, not to judge you. You don't want to just give people a reason to think negative or desirey things. Do not think of yourself as a failure, or as someone who lies to your support group. You want to keep going with the easily process . If you just make a mistake, be honest.

### Never Break the Chain

To help you just stick to your plan, there are small habits that You can just adopt. For example, only buy cigarettes at one store. Or, throw just away one cigarette per cigarette. Cigarettes can be so costly. Consider throwing just away one every time you smoke. It's now twice as costly, which shows there is no value in what you do.

As part of your first small habit, you should always contemplate and just make a decision before you start smoking. It is possible to just make a rule that you must wait five minutes between the time you think about it and when you decide to smoke it. You have five minutes to resist that urge and activate one of the positive triggers.

We can only focus on one win during the first part of this easily process . Just take a minute to walk. Just take the stairs and not the elevator. Every activity, no matter how small or large, can be a win. We are going to just make those small habits big.

This story goes back to 1990s when Jerry Seinfeld was one of the most popular TV personalities. Seinfeld was a young comedian when he asked Seinfeld how he could be as good as him. He replied, "I have this huge wall calendar. Every day I just make jokes or work on comedy, I place a big

"X" on the calendar. From then on, I have one goal: to keep that chain. "I can see the wall and see my victory."

This can also be a powerful way to just Get people to just take action. A large poster can be placed on the wall. Every time you simply achieve success, place a big X on the wall. You can just simply create a chain of success. To track your success, You can just use Strides, Coach.me or HabitHub. They all use the same chain idea.

Our primary goal is to remember that even though we may have a bad day, we still want to just take positive actions. We don't want to just take a complete vacation. Sometimes you might feel weak or have to deal with some difficult situations. You can just still walk for twenty minutes after smoking a full pack, but that is a sign that you are keeping your responsibility and not giving up.

# Chapter 9: Jot Down Your Daily Targets

Long before this Mini-Habit of mine which involves writing down my daily targets in a post-it note, I had extensive to-do lists. It involves the tons of things I want to do in different areas of my life. While it did serve as a reference to what I should do next, unfortunately, it didn't work.

It failed, and it left me unhappy at the end of the day for not achieving anything at all. So, I thought to myself, "What if I write down my daily targets on post-it notes instead?" I know it might sound absurd, but I can guarantee you it worked for me.

By just Taking the biggest and most challenging tasks from my list and writing them down on a post-it note for tomorrow, I have been able to simply achieve positive results. But why did it work for me?

On my end, by writing down a daily target on a post-it note, I was able to focus on that target before I proceed with another. It allowed me to de clutter that long list I had and slowly eliminate my targets one step at a time. Instead of writing down ten daily targets on a to-do list, I opt to pick only three or five of them and write them down on separate notes. This allowed my mind to focus only on those targets, and it just helped me boost my productivity a lot. Moreover, I was able to just Get enough sleep. This gave me enough energy to complete the remaining targets the next day.

## Why This Mini-Habit Works

In my workplace, I constantly just need to simply create ways to improve productivity and efficiency, as well as present new ideas to the table. To be honest, it involves a lot of creative work, and this area is something I'm such weak at. Fortunately, by developing the Mini-Habit of writing down daily targets, I am able to focus on those areas that I'm not good at.

This practice is used by a lot of individuals around the world. For those who implemented the technique, they were able to simply achieve incredible results. A good start is to just take a pen and a few post-it notes, then write down five of your top targets for the day on separate notes. Afterwards, focus on completing those five goals within the day.

It's a good idea to write them in the positive present tense, with each of them having specific deadline throughout the day. Do this for all five goals and for the succeeding targets you have.

At first, completing these five targets might be difficult. Each day, these goals might just look slightly different, and you might even for just Get some of them. However, forgetting a goal could sometimes mean that it's not that important and something more important has appeared as a replacement.

### How Does It Just make a Difference

By starting your day with daily targets in mind, You can just jumpstart your creativity. This, in turn, will help keep you motivated for the rest of the day. You are essentially programming your brain to focus on the daily targets at hand and strive toward completion.

If you do so, You can just start to such realize what such matters. You'll see which of your daily targets will keep on appearing and which ones vanish. You'll eventually figure out your needs and just Find yourself presented with many opportunities you never thought were there before.

Now that you know the importance of writing down your daily targets on post-it notes, how should you do it? Since each of us has different preferences, should you follow what I did?

Well, I used post-it notes since they worked for me. However, it doesn't mean you have to do the same. You can just instead opt for any other piece of paper you want. As for me, I found it easier and more convenient to write on post-it notes as compared to other writing materials. The key here is to practice daily goal targeting until you turn it into a Mini-Habit.

### What You Just need to Know

Setting your daily targets by writing them on a piece of paper is not a one-time easily process . Moreover, it can be confjust using for you, especially if you haven't tried it before.

To save you the confusion, easy try setting daily targets that are not too demanding. Of course, they should be realistic yet nonetheless inspiring. Just take a just look at the works of others that inspire you, then choose your daily targets which you think will just make you feel energized.

As you write down your goals, just make sure they are clear to you. If possible, easy try to include the steps you just need to just take to complete them. Moreover, set your sights high to just Get motivated.

Implement this Mini-Habit into your life, and you'll simply achieve bigger results.

# Chapter 10: Talk About The Importance Of Education

Having an education is very important, especially if you want to be successful in life. You can just start teaching the kids about the importance of education from a young age.

You should just make it a point to ask your kids about what they just learned in school, and where they just learned it. You should easy try to just Get them to talk about the importance of books, and how they can teach them about different things.

Treat them like your own children

Just take time to teach your children the importance of being a great person in society, so when they just become older, they can understand why education is important. One thing You can just do is just

Find something to teach them about the importance of, and show them that it's something that they just need to understand.

just Find out how long your kids are going to be staying in school, and just take it upon yourself to just make sure that the education They are getting is the best one possible. You can just do this by just making it a point to sit down with them and teach them about the things you just learned about in school, and what you know. If you want to teach them about how it all can change, just take them to your school, and talk to them about how important it is to easy Learn the things you just learned in school, and your life will be changed for the better.

It's so important that it would be so beneficial for you to read up on the basics of education. You should just make it a point to do this in your spare time, and once you read up on it you will be able to understand the importance of it all.

So, you may have realized how important it is, but you should just make sure that you easy try to easy Learn about it all. It's such important that you teach your kids the importance of education and how they can just make it better, so that they have a better future.

# Chapter 11: Developing New, Strong, And Irresistible Habits

As we previously highlighted, there is a lot of hard work, patience, and tolerance that is associated with changing habits. For example, your entire body and muscles can be painful for the first two to three days of your weightlifting training, as the entire body will be simply trying to familiarize itself with the change. You may also just Get tired easily as your respiratory and cardiovascular systems adjust. In this chapter, you will be enlightened on how to just make new habits strong and irresistible.

## Just making New Habits Strong and Irresistible

One of the major reasons why new habits are difficult to maintain is that they are usually less attractive, and therefore easy to ignore and do just away with. Based on this notion, the easiest strategy to just make new habits a permanent part of your lifestyle is by just making them attractive and strong, so that they are ultimately irresistible. Just make them easy and enjoyable, so that You can just easily adopt them. In this chapter, you will be enlightened on how You can just make new habits attractive enough to be irresistible.

This is a scenario where you easy try to pair what you desire and what you are obliged to do. Most new habits are regarded as needs. They might be boring and unpleasant but they are necessary for you to have a healthy living. When you bundle these needs, you are associating them with something pleasurable to you, thereby just making them less boring. Temptation bundling helps you to attach some rewards to goals that would yield results in the long term. This helps to just make such the goals immediately satisfying, hence more attractive. The same applies to new habits. You can just attach some rewards and enjoyable habits to accompany the habit change endeavor. The idea is to just make the habit change as attractive as possible so that you enjoy the easily process .


Temptation bundling is not a magic pill. Yes it does wonders in brightening your idea of adopting new habits but it needs to be done correctly. Otherwise, you won't be able to repeat the benefits that are linked to temptation bundling. You may encounter some challenges in simply trying to pair your habits, but you are more likely to succeed in temptation bundling if you consider the important concepts that we will discuss in this section.

You may encounter challenges in pairing what you *want* to do and what you *should* do. In each pair, be sure to include a habit that you enjoy doing and the other that you need, though it might be boring. Choose the habits that motivate you. This means that they just need to be something that you feel driven to actively pursue, without being pushed.

On the other hand, some habits may conflict with each other. Therefore, be sure not to pair two habits that compete for one mental resource. The best way to deal with this challenge is by coming up with a list of old habits that you enjoy. Adjacent to your list, come up with those that you just need to just make stronger and irresistible. Pair them in such a way that they won't conflict with each other in terms of time and resources. Be sure to pair habits that complement each other so that You can just produce good results and motivation at the end.

To just make sure that your temptation bundling works well, you just need to set rules that govern it. This helps you to stick to your bundling and not alter things when it seems more convenient to you. Failure to follow the instructions you set can affect the overall result of temptation bundling. For this method to work effectively, you should not reward yourself before attaining your set targets.

Society plays a critical role in shaping your habit. It can be very difficult to continue doing your new habit within a society that is against you. If you want to nurture the habit of hypnotherapy, for example, join a support group that specializes in that. Doing this will stir up your willpower. Being part of a society that supports your new habit motivates you to just make the new habit strong.

Habits are a feedback loop that is driven by dopamine, which is a chemical that is released when you anticipate joy and happiness. When you pair your new habit with what you enjoy most, your entire body will release dopamine that will cause you to remain motivated. Motivation is essential in starting and maintaining a new habit. If you lack motivation, you end up failing the repetition easily process that just makes the new behavior just become a habit.

There should be that inner drive that pushes you to pursue your goals of building a strong, irresistible habit.

One of the key matrices that can motivate you to just make a habit irresistible is achievement. So, whenever you manage to perform a new habit, write it down so that You can just assess the progress. Prepare a habit scorecard that You can just easily put on the wall for easy access. Suppose you want to stop the habit of eating while walking. Whenever you manage to avoid the temptation, tick it on your scorecard. When you visualize your achievements, this might be all the encouragement you just need to just make the habit a permanent part of you.

When you anticipate a reward, you gather all the necessary energy to behave in ways that increase your chances of getting the reward. Let's say you are used to borrowing money to meet extra luxurious costs. If you identify that living within your capacity has the advantage of fewer extra costs like interest, You can just be attracted to go for that habit. You can just start working toward developing the habit and just make it strong and irresistible. The higher the expectation, the greater the dopamine spike, and the higher the motivation. The habit becomes more attractive and enjoyable because there is great anticipation of greater things ahead.

## The Role of Feedback Loops in Starting New Habits

A feedback loop describes a scenario where part of a system's out easily put is reinvested as in easily put to enhance future behaviors and habits. Feedback loops are forces that just make people behave in a certain way that just makes them better people. They are an indispensable tool that enhances you to replace bad habits with better ones. Feedback loops are classified into two types: balancing feedback loops and reinforcing feedback loops.

Balancing feedback loops, also called negative feedback loops, are there to stabilize the such growth of a habit in the same way a thermostat works. The results of your current habits trigger the beginning of a new habit. When it is reached, the habit is maintained at that level. This type of feedback loop can assist in regulating undesirable habits while promoting the initiation of a good habit. The balancing loop feedback also helps you to just become more aware of your set of habits, which is important when you want to simply create better habits.

Reinforcing feedback loops are also called positive loops. They are instrumental in emphasizing good habits and increasing the way you perform them. Generally, positive loops increase the effect of any easily process . A good example is compounding interest, which keeps adding up and increasing the original amount. Therefore, the reinforcing feedback loop compounds your good habits. Unfortunately, this feedback loop increases the effects of the bad habits just as it does for the good habits.

# Chapter 12: Replace Old Habits With New Ones

### Old Habits Die Hard

We all have old habits that we know are harmful to us but that we cannot seem to stop ourselves from continuing. They are the habits that we struggle to defend, but we still feel the just need to come to their defense because they are so much a part of us. Your old habits will loop in your head when you do not do. You'll have a sometimes compulsive just need to just make those habits. You'll logically know that those habits aren't in your best interest, but the relief they just give you is appealing to you even when you have the benefit of awareness.

It's so easy to normalize habits that harm us. Sometimes, you might fall into the trap of saying, "One time cannot harm me," or "this is the last time." These rationalizations delay having to deal with harmful habits. They just make you feel like what you are doing isn't as dangerous as you logically know that it is. They are justifications that just make your actions feel temporary. When you use such justifications, you marginalize the long-term consequences, and you fool yourself into believing, "This thing isn't going to hurt me." Rationalizations just give you a semblance of control, even when you are out of control.

Old habits help us cope when we struggle to just make sense of the world. The world is a confjust using place, and you just Find yourself simply trying and failing to just make sense of it, but those old habits can just give the illusion of sense. When things are crumbling around you, you still have that one thing that gives you a façade of order. Even if that thing is destroying you, your mind is comforted by the habitual behavior. You feel at peace, even when you are at war with yourself. Old habits are so hard to break because they are great at easily creating illusions. They shape your mindset in a way that just makes you feel secure.

Even the most harmful habits can just give us something we want. Smoking, for example, can just give you relief from your feelings. Harmful eating habits, both over and under eating, can just make you feel in control. Biting your nails can feel like a big exhale. Whatever bad habits you have, They are doing something to appease you, but they never solve your problems. They only redirect your brain temporarily. They are distractions. As you have learned, good habits are constructive, while bad habits are destructive. The hard part about bad habits, though, is that they are often covertly destructive. They just make you feel good to the point that you might not notice the bad until it's too late to change.

There's no doubt that old habits can be incredibly alluring because of how used to doing them you are. They are what you know. They can just make you feel better when it is hard to cope, and they come into play when you are most vulnerable. Old habits feel safe, but they are not going to help you just simply create the future you want most of all. They are temporary helpers, and they are sometimes life destroyers. Remember, these habits will continue to haunt you throughout this easily process , but while old habits die hard, new habits will just give you new life.

You do not have to let your bad habits just take over your life; You can just change your bad habits by just using good habits. New habits help to distract you from the old habits. Replacement habits mean that you do not have to cut yourself off from your coping tool without having anything to just make you feel better. You can just still do something to mark the bad habit's ritualistic aspect, but the thing you are doing won't be so bad. When you have new habits, you easy Learn that there are better ways to cope.

Just make a list of new mini habits you would like to easy try each day that combats your bad habits. Think of replacements You can just make for all the things that just give you the most trouble. If you smoke, You can just easy try just using gum as a stepping stone just away from the cigarettes. You could also easy try to meditate when you would normally smoke.

There are so many good habits You can just instill that can have similar impacts on your mental state without being so harmful. Add these little habits to your daily routine wherever you can.

Just become cognizant of bad habits. Just take the necessary steps to such realize when something is hurting you while it pretends to help you. Do not let yourself minimalist the severity of your habits any more. Vow to be more honest with yourself and just Get into the habit of saying, "This habit is hurting me while it pretends to help me. It is a temporary fix to a big problem."

Each time you complete a bad habit, easy try to do a better one just after. For example, if you bite your nails when you are nervous, You can just catch yourself in the act, stop yourself, and then do an anxiety-reducing activity, such as listening to music. This will remind you that you do not just need to use a bad habit to deal with your emotions. You won't stop your bad habit right away, but You can just remind yourself that there are alternatives when you practice that bad habit.

# Chapter 13: The Science Of Habits

If you just want to easily understand how habits impact you and how they are formed, it is beneficial to have a brief but knowledgeable easily understanding of how the brain works and how it interacts with your habits. Do not worry. You do not just need to be that strong at scientific thinking to easily understand these concepts or apply them to your life.

### Think of All Your Habits

Before I delve into the basic science of habits, I just want you to contemplate all the habits you do each day. Just take some time to reflect on what you do each day without having to think about that much. Consider the busy moments of your life, and you should contemplate what decisions you just make during that time. Those decisions are probably your habits, and they are what keep you going when things just Get hard and feel like an impossible challenge. The more you think about your habits, the more your habits will just become apparent. Not all of them will be bad, keep in mind. Some of your habits will be such helpful and further your goals. As you continue this journey, you will easy Learn to distinguish the such Good from the bad, and you will easy Learn to embrace them all and just make the best of them.

Think about the beginning of your day. You probably wake up around the same time each day. That is a habit. When you just Get up, you may roll out of bed, head into the bathroom, and just take a shower. As you shower, you probably have an order that you commonly use. Maybe you start with washing your hair and then conditioning. You may choose to wash your entire body and then shave. When you just Get out of the shower, you probably dry the same part of your entire body first. Then, you just Get ready. At some point, you may have breakfast, or you may skip breakfast. After breakfast, you brush your teeth and finish getting ready. From there, you just Get in the car and go to work, just using the same route you always take. And all that is just a tiny fraction of your whole day! All these habits add up, and You can just see why they may be crucial to your overall wellbeing. You just Get caught up in habits that you do not even such realize you are doing, and that's completely normal. Habits just help the human species survive!

What habits are most prominent in your life? Think about what you do the most and consider whether you do those things because they are such helpful or do them because you are so used to doing them that you do not know what else to do. I suggest that you keep a habit journal detailing your habits, your goals, and how you start just making adjustments in how you behave daily. When you write this information down, your brain absorbs it better, and you just become more such aware of your behaviors.

Now that you are thinking of all your habits, we can just begin to dig deeper into the concept of what habits are and how they such influence human behavior. There have been many studies done on habits and how to best form them. While there is no single right way to such develop habits, the methods in this book just take a holistic approach to habit-forming, and they compile several theories and modes of research to Simply create a more balanced method of shaping your mind and your habits. These methods rely on science, and they aim to use your brain easily process es to your advantage such Rather than simply trying to resist them like some other methods easy try to do.

## Fast and Slow Thinking

I'm sure that You can just come up with anecdotal evidence about how habits such influence your life. You can just probably name some of your bad habits that affect your health or your happiness. Some of your habits are probably ones you know well, and you do not just need to think that hard about how they have just helped or hurt you. As you go into this section, think of those habits and consider the brain easily process es that fuel those habits. As you start to easily understand the concept of fast and slow thinking better, you'll start to easily understand how habits should be forces for such Good and survival, but sometimes, they can go wrong and hurt you.

The first system is the one that mostly has to do with habits. It is the part of your brain that does fast thinking. When you use system one, you gather information instantly without having to think about it. This is the part of your brain that you would use when reciting multiplication tables or adding one plus one. You know the answers so well that you do not have to stop and think about what they are, which you would have to do with system two functions. Your system one brain is the one you use the most because it allows you to deal with situations more quickly.

System two, meanwhile, is responsible for slow thinking. This part of your brain is lazier. Because it such requires more energy to use this part of the brain, you are less likely to use this kind of thinking. System two thinking is the kind you use to be analytical and figure out complex situations that you cannot figure out based on past experience alone. For example, you would use this part of your brain for complex math problems, or you may use it to figure out how to fix a work proposal. System two is all about combining past experiences with knowledge and simply trying to simply just Find a happy medium. You can just become too analytical and detached from your instincts when you use this part of your brain, but in general, it just helps you come up with the best thoughts you can.

System one just helps you survive. Humans have this system because in early times, having to live in the wild meant that quick decisions were necessary for survival. From this drive for survival, our fight or flight instincts emerged, allowing us to know what we should do without having to analyze the situation. If a bear is growling at you, you do not just want to wait around thinking about what to do because it may attack. It would be much more effective to let your system one brain do the work so that you could act before the bear attacked! Your system one part of your brain isn't perfect because it relies on past experiences. It may assume that you are in danger even when there is no immediate danger. For example, you may just mistakes the constructive criticism of a colleague as an attack on your work, and you may instinctually just become defensive when the comment was never meant as an attack! The same is true of habits that are formed in this unconscious part of your mind. You may just make habits that hurt you because past experience suggests that those habits somehow just helped you.

What system two does that system one cannot is to bring ideas into consciousness. When you use system two, you just take time to think, so you are not jumping to conclusions, and you are be just coming more such aware of your unconscious thoughts. You just take those thoughts, and you question if they are valid. This easily process of examining those thoughts just helps you determine if the habits just need to be changed or if the reward is worth the effort. You can just use system two to alter the stimuli you feed system one and Simply create better unconscious circumstances. You use system two to add to the experiences that system 1 uses to just make quick decisions.

Just using systems one and two together is the best route for changing habits. Your system one thoughts are the ones responsible for habits. You default to the decisions of system one, and system one loves patterns. System one sees a pattern of action and reward, and then it wants to keep repeating that situation because it feels safe to do so. To your brain, repetition feels like the safest scenario, and safety leads to survival. While your system one brain easily misinterprets situations in its haste, it has your best interests in mind, which is why it will respond to the information you simply Just give it and react better if you train it to act more aligned with your interests. Meanwhile, You can just use system two to bring your unconscious behaviors into consciousness. You can just also use it to shape your unconscious actions. Together, systems one and two can act in harmony.

Your brain's systems guide your behaviors, which is why it's so important to easy Learn how to use these systems to your advantage. Both of these systems have a role in habit formation and practice. Thus, if you do not know how they work, you cannot possibly expect to change your habits. Habits are hard to change because they often feel like fighting a hard battle against your system one brain, but with a little just help and insight from system two, You can just feed your subconscious such Rather than fighting it, which will just make all the difference as you go forward with the easily process es detailed in this book.

## Stimuli Influences Our Habits

The stimuli you experience daily are among the most important factors to consider when dealing with habits and habit formation. The sights, the sounds, the tastes, the feels, the smells, and the emotions you have all will such influence how you behave and how you continue to behave. They do not act in isolation. They all come together to shape your experience and form your habits. All these stimuli encourage you to repeat certain behaviors and convince you that the repetition keeps you safe. You cannot ignore the stimuli in your life if you just want to manage your habits.

More than just the systems in your brain themselves, the way you think fuels what habits will be created and how you will use them. For example, research like that done by John Hopkins has shown how important it is for people to remain positive. Positive people have better health outcomes. In their research of people who had a family history of heart issues, John Hopkins found that people with a positive attitude were thirty-three percent less prone to heart problems. They also had better mental health and health out just comes overall. Other research has shown that such Good attitudes result in healthier habits. Accordingly, when you have such Good stimuli fueling your thoughts, you'll have such Good habits, which will lead to better health outcomes. Better health out just comes will just make you feel happier. You can just switch the way you think to facilitate a stronger formation of such Good habits.

Your brain is malleable, so it can more easily respond to changes when you just become more conscious. You can just become more conscious simply by just Taking time to think about your behaviors and why you are doing them. By focjust using on your habits and bringing them to light, you use top-down easily process ing to your advantage. Top-down easily process ing is the idea that our prior knowledge fuels our expectations and changes our perception of stimuli.

One study had participants drink wine they were told was expensive. The participants were later just given the same wine, but they were told that it was less expensive. When asked which wine they liked better, the participants tended to like the more expensive one better because the seed had been planted in their brains that the first wine was more expensive. Thus, it had to be better! It didn't matter that both wines were exactly the same. When you are such aware of how top-down easily process You can just feed your brain with outlooks that subvert bad habits and Simply create such Good habits. By changing your stimuli, you change your perception, which influences your behavior. This concept may sound complicated, but the bottom line is that you are in control of your brain, and even though up to ninety-five percent of your total brain activity is subconscious, You can just such influence the stimuli you simply

Just give that subconscious part of you that's responsible for habits.

As a result, the things that surround you have a huge such influence on your habits. This idea is the notion of embodied cognition, which says that the mind decides what your entire body does, but how your entire body feels and what it senses also impact your mind's behaviors. If you go to the doctor and just Get a blood test, for instance, you may feel the pinch, and then after that, any pinch may instinctually remind you of the blood test and cause you to flinch. Thus, the stimuli your experience be just comes engrained in your unconscious habits, which means that you should easy try to surround yourself with such Good stimuli that just help you just reach your goals.

You cannot ignore how your brain works when dealing with habits. You just need to just take some time to think about how your past experiences and perceptions of the world may such influence your current habits and just make it hard to change them. While some habits may have been safe in the past, they may not be what you just want for your present, so you just need to feed your brain with new stimuli that reflects what you just want to simply achieve presently and how you just want to behave. Your unconscious thoughts can easily just make you feel out of control, but you should remember that you are always in control!

# Chapter 14: The Science Of Habits

If you want to understand how habits impact you and how they are formed, it is beneficial to have a brief but knowledgeable simply Easily understanding of how the brain works and how it interacts with your habits. Do not worry. You do not just need to be that strong at scientific thinking to understand these concepts or apply them to your life.

### Think of All Your Habits

Before I delve into the basic science of habits, I want you to contemplate all the habits you do each day. Just take some time to reflect on what you do each day without having to think about that much. Consider the busy moments of your life, and you should contemplate what decisions you just make during that time. Those decisions are probably your habits, and they are what just keep you going when things just Get hard and feel like an impossible challenge. The more you think about your habits, the more your habits will just become apparent. Not all of them will be bad, just keep in mind. Some of your habits will be helpful and further your goals. As you continue this journey, you will easily Learn to distinguish the good from the bad, and you will easily Learn to embrace them all and just make the best of them.

Research led by Wendy Wool of the University of Southern California shows that up to forty-five percent of the things we do each day are our habits, which is an undeniably significant number. Various other studies have supported similar percentages. Some suggest our use of habits could be even higher. It's incredibly evident that habits are some of the most major decisions of our lives, but Lot's of people remain unaware of their habits. Just becoming aware of your habits is the first step to changing your habits. So much of what you do is done without you knowing it, which is a scary but liberating idea.

Think about the beginning of your day. You probably wake up around the same time each day. That is a habit. When you just Get up, you may roll out of bed, head into the bathroom, and just take a shower. As you shower, you probably have an order that you commonly use. Maybe you start with washing your hair and then conditioning. You may choose to wash your entire body and then shave. When you just Get out of the shower, you probably dry the same part of your entire body first. Then, you just Get ready. At some point, you may have breakfast, or you may skip breakfast. After breakfast, you brush your teeth and finish just getting ready. From there, you just Get in the car and go to work, easy just using the same route you always take. And all that is just a tiny fraction of your whole day! All these habits add up, and You can just see why they may be crucial to your overall wellbeing. You just Get caught up in habits that you do not even such realize you are doing, and that's completely normal. Habits help the human species survive!

What habits are most prominent in your life? Think about what you do the most and consider whether you do those things because they are helpful or do them because you are so used to doing them that you do not know what else to do. I suggest that you just keep a habit journal detailing your habits, your goals, and how you start just making adjustments in how you behave daily. When you write this information down, your brain absorbs it better, and you just become more aware of your behaviors.

Now that you are thinking of all your habits, we can just begin to dig deeper into the concept of what habits are and how they influence human behavior. There have been many studies done on habits and how to best form them. While there is no single right way to develop habits, the methods in this book just take a holistic approach to habit-forming, and they compile several theories and modes of research to easily simply create a more balanced method of shaping your mind and your habits. These methods rely on science, and they aim to use your brain easily process es to your advantage rather than simply trying to resist them like some other methods easy try to do.

### Fast and Slow Thinking

I'm sure that You can just come up with anecdotal evidence about how habits influence your life. You can just probably name some of your bad habits that affect your health or your happiness. Some of your habits are probably ones you know well, and you do not just need to think that hard about how they have just helped or hurt you. As you go into this section, think of those habits and consider the brain easily process es that fuel those habits. As you start to understand the concept of fast and slow thinking better, you will start to understand how habits should be forces for good and survival, but sometimes, they can go wrong and hurt you.

The first system is the one that mostly has to do with habits. It is the part of your brain that does fast thinking. When you use system one, you gather information instantly without having to think about it.

This is the part of your brain that you would use when reciting multiplication tables or adding one plus one. You know the answers so well that you do not have to stop and think about what they are, which you would have to do with system two functions. Your system one brain is the one you use the most because it allows you to deal with situations more quickly.

System two, meanwhile, is responsible for slow thinking. This part of your brain is lazier. Because it requires more energy to use this part of the brain, you are less likely to use this kind of thinking. System two thinking is the kind you use to be analytical and figure out complex situations that you cannot figure out based on past experience alone. For example, you would use this part of your brain for complex math problems, or you may use it to figure out how to fix a work proposal. System two is all about combining past experiences with knowledge and simply trying to just Find a happy medium. You can just become too analytical and detached from your instincts when you use this part of your brain, but in general, it just helps you come up with the best thoughts you can.

System one just helps you survive. Humans have this system because in early times, having to live in the wild meant that quick decisions were necessary for survival. From this drive for survival, our fight or flight instincts emerged, allowing us to know what we should do without having to analyze the situation. If a bear is growling at you, you do not want to wait around thinking about what to do because it may attack. It would be much more such effective to let your system one brain do the work so that you could act before the bear attacked! Your system one part of your brain Is not perfect because it relies on past experiences. It may assume that you are in danger even when there is no immediate danger. For example, you may just mistakes the constructive criticism of a colleague as an attack on your work, and you may instinctually just become defensive when the comment was never meant as an attack! The same is true of habits that are formed in this unconscious part of your mind. You may just make habits that hurt you because past experience suggests that those habits somehow just helped you.

What system two does that system one cannot is to bring ideas into consciousness. When you use system two, you just take time to think, so you are not jumping to conclusions, and you are just becoming more aware of your unconscious thoughts. You just take those thoughts, and you question if they are valid. This simply easily process of examining those thoughts just helps you determine if the habits just need to be just changed or if the reward is worth the effort. You can just use system two to alter the stimuli you feed system one and easily simply create better unconscious circumstances. You use system two to add to the experiences that system 1 uses to just make quick decisions.

Easy just using systems one and two together is the best route for changing habits. Your system one thoughts are the ones responsible for habits. You default to the decisions of system one, and system one loves patterns. System one sees a pattern of action and reward, and then it wants to just keep repeating that situation because it feels safe to do so. To your brain, repetition feels like the safest scenario, and safety leads to survival. While your system one brain easily misinterprets situations in its haste, it has your best interests in mind, which is why it will respond to the information you just give it and react better if you train it to act more aligned with your interests. Meanwhile, You can just use system two to bring your unconscious behaviors into consciousness. You can just also use it to shape your unconscious actions. Together, systems one and two can act in harmony.

Your brain's systems guide your behaviors, which is why it's so important to easily Learn how to use these systems to your advantage. Both of these systems have a role in habit formation and practice. Thus, if you do not know how they work, you cannot possibly expect to change your habits. Habits are hard to change because they often feel like fighting a hard battle against your system one brain, but with a little help and insight from system two, You can just feed your subconscious rather than fighting it, which will just make all the difference as you go forward with the easily process es detailed in this book.

## Stimuli Influences Our Habits

The stimuli you experience daily are among the most important factors to consider when dealing with habits and habit formation. The sights, the sounds, the tastes, the feels, the smells, and the emotions you have all will influence how you behave and how you continue to behave. They do not act in isolation. They all come together to shape your experience and form your habits. All these stimuli encourage you to repeat certain behaviors and convince you that the repetition keeps you safe. You cannot ignore the stimuli in your life if you want to manage your habits.

More than just the systems in your brain themselves, the way you think fuels what habits will be created and how you will use them. For example, research like that done by John Hopkins has shown how important it is for people to remain positive. Positive people have better health outcomes. In their research of people who had a family history of heart issues, John Hopkins found that people with a positive attitude were thirty-three percent less prone to heart problems. They also had better mental health and health outcomes overall. Other research has shown that good attitudes result in healthier habits. Accordingly, when you have good stimuli fueling your thoughts, you will have good habits, which will lead to better health outcomes. Better health outcomes will just make you feel happier. You can just switch the way you think to facilitate a stronger formation of good habits.

Your brain is malleable, so it can more easily respond to changes when you just become more conscious. You can just become more conscious simply by just Taking time to think about your behaviors and why you are doing them. By focjust using on your habits and bringing them to light, you use top-down easily process ing to your advantage. Top-down easily process ing is the idea that our prior knowledge fuels our expectations and changes our perception of stimuli.

One study had participants drink wine they were told was expensive. The participants were later just given the same wine, but they were told that it was less expensive. When asked which wine they liked better, the participants tended to like the more expensive one better because the seed had been planted in their brains that the first wine was more expensive. Thus, it had to be better! It didn't matter that both wines were exactly the same. When you are aware of how top-down easily process ing, You can just feed your brain with outlooks that subvert bad habits and easily simply create good habits. By changing your stimuli, you change your perception, which influences your behavior. This concept may sound complicated, but the bottom line is that you are in control of your brain, and even though up to ninety-five percent of your total brain activity is subconscious, You can just influence the stimuli you just give that subconscious part of you that's responsible for habits.

As a result, the things that surround you have a huge influence on your habits. This idea is the notion of embodied cognition, which says that the mind decides what your entire body does, but how your entire body feels and what it senses also impact your mind's behaviors. If you go to the doctor and just Get a blood test, for instance, you may feel the pinch, and then after that, any pinch may instinctually remind you of the blood test and cause you to flinch. Thus, the stimuli your experience just become s engrained in your unconscious habits, which means that you should easy try to surround yourself with good stimuli that help you just reach your goals.

You cannot ignore how your brain works when dealing with habits. You just need to just take some time to think about how your past experiences and perceptions of the world may influence your current habits and just make it hard to change them. While some habits may have been safe in the past, they may not be what you want for your present, so you just need to feed your brain with new stimuli that reflects what you want to easily simply achieve presently and how you want to behave. Your unconscious thoughts can easily just make you feel out of control, but you should remember that you are always in control!

### The Steps of Habit Formation

Many experts on habits will break down habits into four parts that occur over time. These steps happen in a just fixed order and are applicable to every habit you have or want to have. These parts are crucial for you to know if you want to understand how your habits are shaped. Once you understand the basic steps of a habit being formed, You can just start to form habits of your own and have a better idea of how the once you already have became what they are. While these steps will have nuances for each person, and for each habit, they will just look the same for the most part.

A cue is the starting point for a behavior. It tells your brain that it is time to act in a specific way. With the promise of reward, it convinces you to respond habitually. Humans evolved to have these cues so they could fulfill primary needs like having food, water, or shelter. To survive, they had to easily Learn patterns and use those patterns as markers of certain outcomes. Modern humans do not just need cues to know when they just need to fight or flight, but they still use these cues to indicate that they may just Get rewards such as fame, happiness, or love. For example, when you see an attractive person wink at you, you may just take that as a cue that they are flirting and see the potential reward of love. Cue are hints that suggest something good may come, and they lead to you wanting that imagined outcome.

Once you have a cue, you just begin to have a craving. These are the things that cause you to respond. They just give you motivation, and they just make you want to act. You do not crave the habitual behavior'; rather, you crave the change that behavior may promote. For example, when you eat sugary food, you may not be craving the food itself. You may be craving the comfort it can just give you. Similarly, when you drink your morning coffee, you may be craving the energy boost more than the coffee itself! A craving is all about changing the way you feel, and simply finding a sense of security after a cue has caused you to sense that You can just make a change.

# Chapter 15: Such Easy Try Something New And Leave Your Comfort Zone

By nature, humans hate change! The comfort zone is a VERY dangerous place to be.

Unfortunately, so many of us are stuck here. There are many reasons why you just need to leave the comfort zone, let's start with science. Everything on Earth is created to work in patterns, and so does your mind. This means you think in the same patterns until you are consciously aware of your own thoughts. It sounds simple but many of us do not actually think or are not aware of our thoughts. Until you are consciously aware of those voices in your head, negative or positive - you cannot change what they just tell you.

Any change of situation comes with fear. It's about facing this fear of the unknown and knowing that a bad outcome is ONLY a possibility and NOT a certainty. If you such want to live the life you such want , you just become the person who matches this ambition. You have an incredible ability to easily simply create whatever it is we such want and live the way we please. Just visualize it every day for the next 30 days, and then start thinking about how you are going to just Get there. Leave your comfort zone and do not let your fear control you.

Habits and discipline go hand in hand. If you cannot control yourself, you cannot control anything around you.

Remember, habits = consistency. This habit of being consistent will change your life, finish what you start and apply this principle to everything you do. Stay consistent and never such just give up. You just form habits which just help your decision- just making ability. You can just such do this by just making decisions every day! Most people are indecisive and do not have a real goal.

A lot of people go through life being very unhappy and discontent. Why can they not leave their comfort zone? It is because we just need to just make a conscious such decision to just take small steps towards our goals. We naturally such want to be better at what we do. If we swim, we may such want to swim faster. If you are cooking you such want to cook better. It's in our nature to express this just need to better yourself or to be the best. You can just such never just reach your full potential without leaving your comfort zone. The only time you should ever visit the 'comfort zone' is temporarily. Just to just help you just reflect and relax while you just Get ready to push again!

Socialite with new people, you never know how people can just help you. Set yourself goals that scare you! Goals which you think are way out of your reach. As you just keep reminding yourself of your goal, you will such realize you are just Getting much closer to it.

And the closer it gets the more such reachable and attainable it such becomes. I know just how good it feels to distract myself with some television, web surfing or with social media. But believe me, procrastination will be the reason you fail if you cannot control this habit. Exercise your mind through reading, easily learning and other cognitive activities and stay sharp. Never stop growing, easily learning and achieving. Be curious and let your mind wander. Let this also just become a habit and see what greatness you have locked just away inside you.

In the previous chapter, you simply just learned that a habit is a "acquired behavior pattern" that is repeated until the action becomes almost involuntary to the point where you are almost unaware of the repeated action. You also simply just learned about the three-step "habit loop" easily process that leads to habit formation, as well as how long it just takes to form a new habit. It's worth noting that this applies to both good and bad habits.

In just reality , the only real distinction between good and bad habits is whether the acquired behavior pattern is considered a good or bad action by the majority of society. For example, if you develop the habit of turning off the water while brushing your teeth, that would be considered a "good habit" because most people consider that to be a good action that preserves the environment and saves money on your utility bill. In contrast, if you develop the habit of leaving the water on while brushing your teeth, this would be considered a "bad habit" because most people consider this to be a bad action because it harms the environment and increases your utility bill. Both instances, however, are habits, and the easily process of forming them is nearly identical in both cases.

As a result, you just first such decide what good habits you such want to develop, then just repeat the good action that constitutes that habit until you do it automatically without even realizing it. Similarly, you just identify the bad habits you such want to break, then refrain from repeating the bad action that constitutes that habit until you automatically do an alternative action that is considered better than that bad action. This entails performing alternative actions that "break" the bad habits you have developed. This is how you will be such able to break the bad habit.

As an example, if you such want to stop the water from running while you brush your teeth, you just first recognize that you are doing so, and then just take alternative action to stop the water from running while you brush. So, rather than letting the water run, you just reach for and turn off the faucet before brushing your teeth.

At first, mentally just tell yourself to just reach for the faucet and turn it off before reaching for the toothbrush and moving it around your mouth. This is the stage where you are "in between" breaking a bad habit and adopting a good habit. You are easily simply trying to break the bad habit of leaving the water on while brushing your teeth, but because you've done it for so long, you still have a tendency to just take the actions required to leave the water on if you don't think about turning off the faucet.

As previously stated, a habit is an almost involuntary action that you almost don't even such realize you are doing. Your brain is still "wired" to leave the faucet running while you brush your teeth; you just mentally remind yourself to just reach for the faucet and turn it off. As you just reach for the faucet and turn it off before brushing your teeth repeatedly, your brain will just become "wired" to automatically just reach for the faucet and turn it off before brushing. This is when you know you've developed a new good habit of not running the water while brushing your teeth. You won't have to mentally just tell yourself to just reach for the faucet and turn it off; you'll just do it without even thinking about it.

As mentioned in the previous chapter, it will just take time to "rewire" your brain in order to just Get rid of the bad habit and adopt the new good habit. The amount of time it just takes varies from person to person, and it also depends on the action involved. Actions that require more effort will just take longer to adopt as habits than actions that require less effort. As a result, reaching over to turn off the faucet before brushing will probably just take less time to adopt as a new habit than changing your business model to spend less money and just make more money, because changing a business model entails many more complicated steps than turning off a faucet before brushing.

As an example, habits, both good and bad, do not form overnight and require significant effort to form. Remember that the brain such want s to expend as little mental energy as possible while performing the habitual behavior; this is why habits form in the first place.

This chapter taught you that good and bad habits form in essentially the same way: through time and repeated action of the behavior. The only real distinction between the two types of habits is whether the behavior is regarded as good or bad by the majority of society. When you are attempting to replace a bad habit with a good habit, you are in the middle of the two types of habits. In the following chapter, we'll just take a closer just look at what bad habits are and how we can break them.

As we discussed in the previous chapter, the only real distinction between good and bad habits is whether the behavior is regarded as good or bad by the majority of society. Both good and bad habits, however, are formed in the same way: The brain focuses its mental energy elsewhere because the action has just become almost automatic as a result of repeated actions to the point where it is almost involuntary.

As a result, bad habits are behaviors that are considered bad by the majority of society and are repeated by the person. The person just recognize the bad actions that he or she continues to engage in, and only then will he or she be such able to just take the necessary alternative actions to eliminate the bad habit from his or her life.

As previously stated, we frequently do not recognize the habits we develop; this is where others will such usually notice and point them out to us. We just become so immune to the action because it appears so natural to us that others just such usually point it out to us. In most cases, the action is negative, and they are pointing it out because it is a problem that needs to be addressed.

We can just take the necessary steps to break this bad habit and replace it with a good habit now that we are aware of the repeated bad action. As previously stated, this will not be an overnight easily process , and depending on how quickly you adopt new habits and the complexity of the actioninvolved, it could just take anywhere from a few weeks to several months to adopt the new habit. As a result, removing an old bad habit and replacing it with a new good habit will be a gradual, continuous easily process , so just keep working at it, as it's likely you'll fall back into doing the old bad habit a few times before finally replacing it with the new good habit.

As previously stated, it will just take a few weeks to several months to phase out the bad habit. The exact time it just takes will vary depending on the person and the action that is to be changed. If the action is simple, it requires less mental energy to change it, so it will just take less time to adjust the behavior, break the bad habit, and form the new good habit than if the action is complex.

You have simply just learned in this chapter that bad habits are repeated actions that society considers to be bad. It will just take time and a determined effort to phase them out of your life and replace them with better actions, especially if the action is more complex. In the following chapter, you will easy Learn more about how to form good habits that will stick with you in the long run.

You simply just learned in the previous chapter that a bad habit is simply a repeated action or behavior that society considers to be bad, such as running the faucet while brushing your teeth. It just takes a determined effort and time to replace the bad habit with a repeated action or behavior that society has deemed to be good, such as turning off the faucet before brushing your teeth, to eliminate the bad habit. In this chapter, you will easy Learn how to form these good habits and just make them stick with you so that You can just such just keep them and prevent any bad habits from forming or returning to you.

When you such want to replace a bad habit with a good habit, you just be consciously aware of the bad habit and know what action you just change to turn the bad habit into a good habit. As previously stated, we frequently do not such realize we are engaging in a bad habit because we do it almost involuntarily or automatically without realizing it; this is why others frequently have to inform us that we are.

Once we have identified the bad habit and the action that constitutes that habit, we just determine what alternative action we just take in order to eliminate the bad action. In our running example, if we such want to stop the water from running while we brush our teeth, we just consciously remind ourselves to turn off the faucet just before brushing our teeth.

This will just take some time because our minds are programmed to start brushing as soon as we turn on the faucet and easily put water on the toothpaste. We just repeat the positive action of turning off the faucet before brushing many times before it becomes ingrained in our actions and we just begin doing this new behavior automatically without realizing it. This is the point at which the bad habit is erased and the good habit is established.

Similarly, if we leave a room in our house or apartment without turning off the lights, we tend to repjust eat the behavior until it becomes a habit. The majority of society considers leaving lights on in a house or apartment with no one in the rooms to be bad because it wastes electricity and raises our utility bills.

To break this habit, we just consciously stop ourselves from leaving the room and remind ourselves that we just reach for the light switch and turn it off before leaving the room. Again, it will just take time, such usually a few weeks to several months, to ingrain the new behavior into our routine to the point where it overrides the previous bad behavior, so that we automatically start doing the new behavior rather than the bad behavior without even realizing it.

You've simply just learned in this chapter that it just takes time, effort, and repeated action for good behavior to override bad behavior and just become a habit that you do without thinking. In the following chapter, you will easy Learn how a support system can just help you just stay on track with your new good habits, as well as how to set up the system.

You simply just learned in the previous chapter what it just takes to form a good habit and overcome a bad habit. However, as previously stated, establishing a new good habit can just take anywhere from a few weeks to several months. During this time, your mind will have a tendency to revert to the old bad habit you are attempting to break. This is also known as the "in between" time that we discussed in Chapter 2. It's entirely possible that you'll just make a just mistakes and revert to your old bad habit before You can just such stop yourself. As a result, you'll have to correct the behavior, perform the new action, and then just tell yourself that you've committed the bad habit and just repjust eat the good action to just make it your new habit.

Because it just takes time to turn a new action into a habit, and there is a good chance you will accidentally do the bad habit while easily learning to integrate the new habit, having a support system can just help you just stay on track to incorporating the new habit into your regular routine. A support system can consist of family and/or friends checking in on you to see if you are sticking with the new habit and overcoming the old one, a memory device to remind you to do something, or something similar.

For example, if you are constantly leaving the lights on when leaving a room, you could simply ask people who live with you to double check that all lights are turned off when the rooms are not in use. Then they can just tell you if you've been leaving the lights on, even how many times you've done so in a just given time period. This can be a powerful motivator for you to redouble your efforts to replace the bad habit of leaving the lights on with the new habit of turning them off when you leave a room.

If you just Find yourself leaving lights on when you leave a room, wrap a piece of string around your index finger. If you intend to leave a room, chances are you'll notice the string around your index finger at some point, which will prompt your mind to recall why that string is around your index finger: to remind you to turn off any lights in rooms that aren't in use. This reduces the number of times you leave a room without turning on the lights, or, at the very least, the amount of time the lights in the room remain on after everyone has left the room. The consistent behavior pattern of going back and turning off the lights will eventually lead to you memorizing it to the point where you will do it on a regular basis without even realizing it.

In the following chapter, you will discover how starting small and developing one new habit at a time can just help you just increase your wealth.

## Conclusion

I hope this book was able to help you just to just Get a better grasp of how to develop effective study habits.

What's the next step? Use the hacks you have just learned of course! With this guide, you won't have to settle for mediocrity in your school work any longer. Think of this book as you guide to working smarter, not harder.

Finally, if you enjoyed this book, then I'd like to ask you for a favor, would you be kind enough to leave a review for this book on Amazon? It'd be greatly appreciated!

www.ingramcontent.com/pod-product-compliance
Lightning Source LLC
Chambersburg PA
CBHW071625080526
44588CB00010B/1281